The Deep Blue Planet

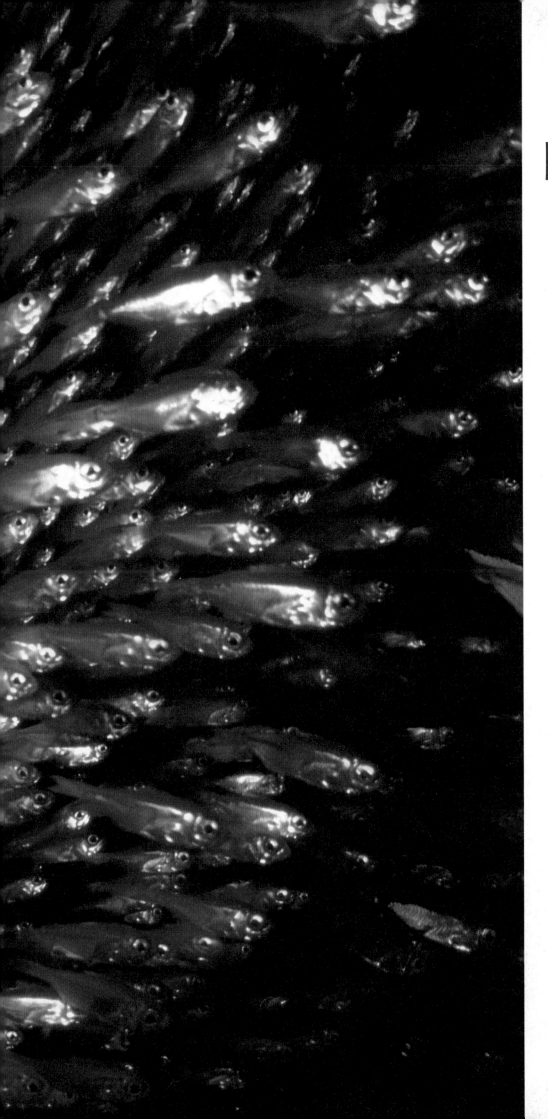

OCEAN ENVIRONMENTS

The Deep Blue Planet

OCEAN ENVIRONMENTS

RENATO MASSA
ENGLISH TRANSLATION BY NEIL FRAZER DAVENPORT

RSVP
RAINTREE
STECK-VAUGHN
PUBLISHERS
The Steck-Vaughn Company

Austin, Texas

© Copyright 1998, English version, Steck-Vaughn Company

© Copyright 1996, Editoriale Jaca Book spa, Milan

Published by Raintree Steck-Vaughn Publishers, an imprint of Steck-Vaughn Company

Editors
Caterina Longanesi, Linda Zierdt-Warshaw, William P. Mara

Design and layout
Jaca Book Design Office

Library of Congress Cataloging-in-Publication Data

Massa, Renato.
    [Ambienti marini. English]
    Ocean environments / Renato Massa ; English translation by Neil Frazer Davenport.
        p.   cm. — (The deep blue planet)
    Includes bibliographical references and index.
    Summary: Surveys the various areas of the ocean environment and the different plant and animal life found in each.
    ISBN 0-8172-4651-7
    1. Marine biology — Juvenile literature.   2. Marine ecology — Juvenile literature.
[1. Marine biology.   2. Marine ecology.   3. Ecology.]   I. Title.   II. Series.
QH91.16.M3613   1998
578.77 — dc21   97–3688
                                                                                                CIP   AC

Printed and bound in the United States
1 2 3 4 5 6 7 8 9 0 WO 01 00 99 98 97

Picture Credits

Photographs
GIANNI ARCUDI, Bergamo: 26-27, 30 (1, 2), 34-35, 40 (2). EDITORIALE JACA BOOK, Milano (DUILIO CITI): 31 (3), 49 (4); (GIORGIO DETTIORI): 10-11, 17, 19, 22-23, 28-29, 32-33, 36-37; (RENATO MASSA): 24, 49 (3, 5); (CARLO SCOTTI): 12. FOTORICERCA DONADONI, Bergamo: 25 (2, 3, 5). MARCO FRIGERIO, Milano: 2-3, 25 (4, 6). MARINA GONANO, Milano: 40 (1). GRAZIA NERI, Milano (NORBERT WU): 41.

Color plates and drawings
EDITORIALE JACA BOOK, Milano (LUISA CITTONE): 27 (9, 10, 11), 34, 35, 37, 44; (MARIA ELENA GONANO): 8, 20-21, 38-39, 42-43; (CARLO JACONO): 46-47; (LORENZO ORLANDI): 12-13, 14-15, 18-19, 45; (GIULIA RE): 16, 22, 26 (1, 2, 3), 48.

CONTENTS

Please note: words in **bold** can also be found in the glossary. They are bold only the first time they appear in the main body of the text.

INTRODUCTION

The oceans and seas are wondrous places of both dark and light, flora and fauna, warm and cold, and life and death. Many regions are still largely unknown to us, so there is little doubt that hundreds of mysteries still lie in their murky depths.

The oceans and seas cover just over 70 percent of the Earth. They have provided us with many pieces to the puzzle of how life began on this planet, since the earliest forms of life were thought to have existed there. The rocks and sediment along the ocean floor have yielded a great deal of fossil evidence over the years.

The value of the oceans and seas is immeasurable. They have given us many useful chemicals and minerals, including bromine, magnesium, and salt, not to mention pearls for jewelry and shells for building material and health supplements. Most experts believe we have not yet realized their full potential in regard to nutrition, though it is believed that humans derive at least 10% of their overall protein from the Earth's waters, either directly or indirectly. Finally, there is the recreational aspect. Activities such as swimming, fishing, boating, diving, and so on, when executed properly and responsibly, provide us with a great deal of pleasure and a measure of relief from the grind of our daily lives.

Sadly, however, we humans have caused some serious damage to the oceans and seas in recent times. Industry is the greatest violator, with over a quarter of a million manufacturing facilities using the great bodies of water as dumping grounds for their often highly dangerous waste products, including mercury, lead, sulfuric acid, and asbestos. In addition, towns and cities regularly dump improperly treated sewage and millions of tons of paper and plastic wastes into rivers, streams, and lakes. Plastics in particular have the potential to remain intact for hundreds of years.

However, we have not yet reached a point of no return, and one of the goals of the *Deep Blue Planet* books is to give you a deeper understanding of—and in turn a deeper appreciation and respect for—the aquatic environments of this world. The more you know about any subject, the greater your appreciation for it will be, and the oceans and seas are in desperate need of increased appreciation. Perhaps someday you will make efforts of your own to preserve these beautiful natural areas and the myriad life forms that thrive within them. If so, you will be helping to guarantee them the bright and vibrant future they so richly deserve.

VARIETY AND EVOLUTION

Marine Ecosystems

The word **environment** would have little meaning on a planet with no life. When you think of the moon or Mars, you may imagine deserts of rocks and dust. You may picture an occasional plain or mountain. Both these places lack the relationships—**symbiosis, parasitism, predation,** and **competition**—that create the conditions for evolution to occur. These relationships create "environments" on a living planet. The environments are **ecosystems** made up of a **biotic community** and **abiotic** features that are tied to the community through the recycling of matter and energy.

On dry land you can experience ecosystems directly. Land ecosystems include forests, prairies, deserts, swamps, and mountains. People know much less about ocean environments, and yet marine ecosystems make up the majority of the **biosphere!**

The dry land part of the biosphere covers about 148 million kilometers^2 (57.2 million mi^2) of land. It has a maximum thickness of about 40 meters (131 ft)—the average height of the trees of the great forests. However, the ocean part of the biosphere covers an area of 361 million kilometers^2 (139.38 mi^2). It has an average depth of about 4,000 meters (13,123 ft).

The Various Types of Ocean Floor

The huge amount of available space in the ocean is demonstrated by something called marine **biodiversity**. Of the 32 major **phyla** of animals, all evolved in the sea. 31 of these are at least partly marine organisms. 14 are solely marine organisms.

Most known plants and animals of today are land species. The insects alone account for about 1.5 million of the known species (if not more). But the variety of basic forms in the marine environment is much greater than that on dry land.

Plant and animal life evolved in the oceans, and there doubtless are many species still awaiting discovery. The number of undiscovered species may in fact be as great as the number of tropical forest species that have yet to be described. This number may be as great as 10 or 20 new species for each species we already know about.

Marine Continuity

Below the flat, unchanging surface of the ocean, water properties decide the environment. Temperatures vary only within a range from about 4°C (39°F) to a little over 30°C (86°F), except in certain exceptional areas. Humidity has no meaning in this environment. Pressure increases with the water depth.

Perhaps the most important factor of the marine environment is the presence of light. Light decreases quickly, making it impossible for plant life to survive at depths greater than 200 meters (656 ft). This is called the limit of the **photic zone**. There is no light at all below 400 meters (1,312 ft). The amount of dissolved oxygen in the water also lessens with depth. In some areas of the deep ocean, oxygen is absent.

Because of differences in conditions, ocean waters worldwide have an amazing variety of organisms. And yet, most of these organisms belong to the same groups, whether they are from the warm tropical waters or the freezing polar seas. In the photic zone, you will find **sponges, cnidarians, ctenophores,** bristleworms, **mollusks,** sea squirts, sea fans, sea stars, **crustaceans,** and fishes. These animals may graze on the sea bed or float and dart at various ocean depths. **Algae** are also in abundance.

The Sea in the History of Life

Life has existed in the oceans for billions of years, perhaps as many as 3.5 billion. However, life appeared on dry land only about 400 million years ago. Thus, marine life has a history almost ten times longer than life on dry land. Marine life is also more complex than life on land.

Life may have first appeared in the sea 3.5 billion years ago. It existed in single-celled form for a long time. The evolution of multi-celled organisms was marked by the appearance of sponges, like these from the tropical seas. In sponges, each cell is identical and feeds individually. However, the colony has a typical appearance that comes from collective activity.

Marine organisms have an incredible variety of physical traits. These traits apply to the 31 surviving phyla plus some extinct species as well. One extinct example is *Xenusion* of the Precambrian Era. This organism lived more than 590 million years ago. *Xenusion* resembled **trilobites**, myriapods, crustaceans, and the **annelid** worms.

During the Cambrian Era (590-500 million years ago), all life on Earth lived in the oceans, and many modern groups of organisms were present back then. These groups include the jellyfishes, sponges, corals, crustaceans, **brachiopods**, **cephalopods**, **gastropods**, and the first **echinoderms**. Among these groups, one of the best known is the aforementioned trilobites. The trilobites were **arthropods**—invertebrates with jointed appendages and a hard exoskeleton. They dominated the seas for about 300 million years, then they disappeared, about 250 million years ago. This group represented about 60% of the animal life of the Cambrian Era. They varied greatly in size, from a few millimeters to 1.5 meters (4.9 ft) in length.

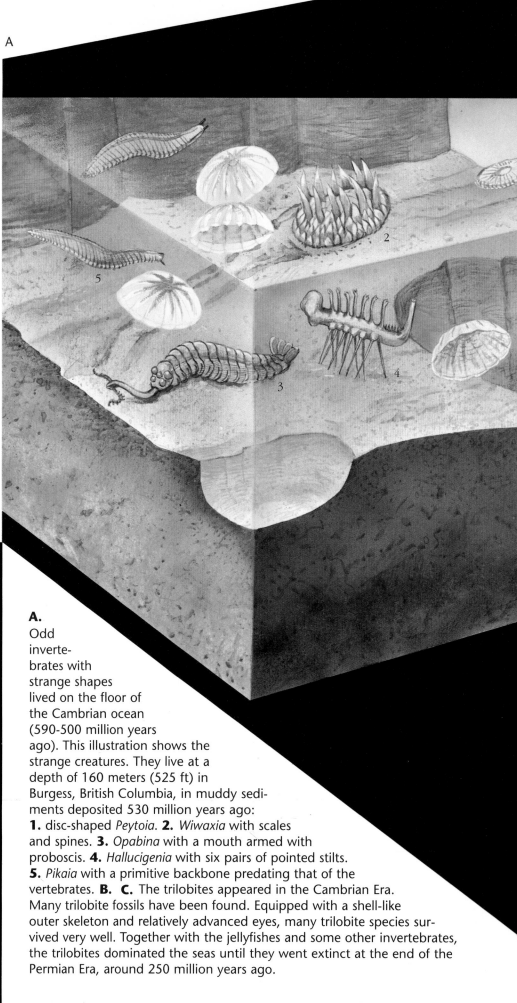

A

B

A. Odd invertebrates with strange shapes lived on the floor of the Cambrian ocean (590-500 million years ago). This illustration shows the strange creatures. They live at a depth of 160 meters (525 ft) in Burgess, British Columbia, in muddy sediments deposited 530 million years ago: **1.** disc-shaped *Peytoia*. **2.** *Wiwaxia* with scales and spines. **3.** *Opabina* with a mouth armed with proboscis. **4.** *Hallucigenia* with six pairs of pointed stilts. **5.** *Pikaia* with a primitive backbone predating that of the vertebrates. **B. C.** The trilobites appeared in the Cambrian Era. Many trilobite fossils have been found. Equipped with a shell-like outer skeleton and relatively advanced eyes, many trilobite species survived very well. Together with the jellyfishes and some other invertebrates, the trilobites dominated the seas until they went extinct at the end of the Permian Era, around 250 million years ago.

C

1

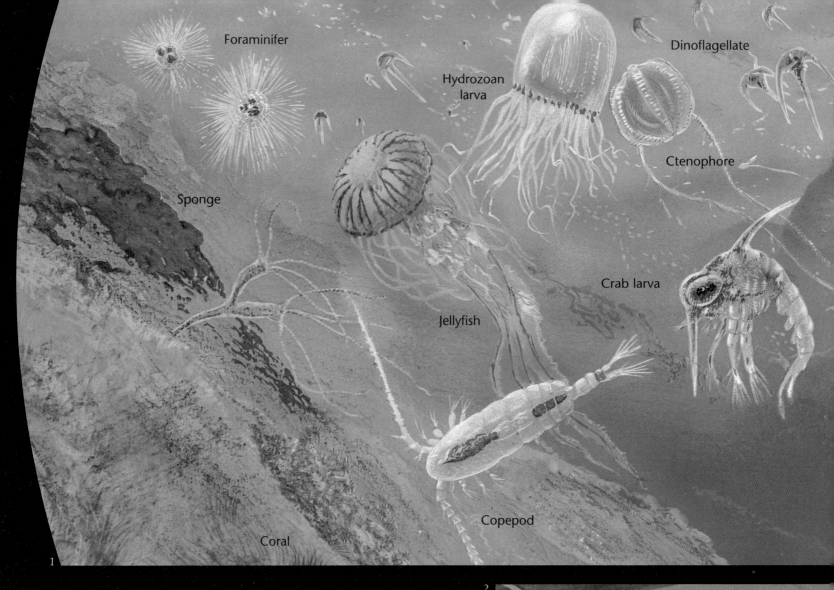

Foraminifer

Dinoflagellate

Hydrozoan
larva

Sponge

Ctenophore

Crab larva

Jellyfish

Copepod

Coral

1

2

Rhamphodaspis

Dinichthys

1. During
the Cambrian
Period, life in the
sea was highly
evolved. This illustra-
tion (animals are not
drawn to scale) shows some
marine invertebrate groups that
have survived. These invertebrates
include foraminifers and dinoflagellates. Both are microscopic protists that
live in the sea and along the coasts. The
ancient sponges formed from colonies of individual cells that existed in the Precambrian Era. Ancient
cnidarians were also present. They included jellyfishes,
ctenophores, ceriantherates, corals, sea anemones,
and hydrozoans, among others. Segmented worms, brachiopods with shells, and crustaceans, such as the copepods
(which are small planktonic organisms), also existed.

Hydrozoan

Sea anemone

Ceriantherate

Brachiopod

Sponge

Worm

Pterychthys

2. In the Devonian Period (410-360 million years ago), the main evolutionary theme was the explosion of a group of fishes having internal skeletons (vertebrates), like *Ramphodaspis*, *Dinichthys*, and *Pterychthys*. These fishes appeared between the end of the Ordovician and the beginning of the Silurian periods (about 450 million years ago). The fishes were placoderms—predators with the front part of their body protected by bony plates. They had a powerful new weapon—an expressed jaw with teeth. At the end of the Devonian Period, the placoderms went extinct. They were replaced by the first modern fishes—those with cartilaginous skeletons, like the sharks, and those with bony skeletons.

RESTING, FLOATING, AND SWIMMING ORGANISMS

neuston

plankton

plankton

nekton

benthos

1

Benthos, or Sea Floor Life

Marine organisms are classified in about forty major groups (**divisions**). Almost one-fourth of these groups belongs to the plant kingdom. Most of the remaining groups belong to the animal kingdom. From an ecological point of view, the simplest way to classify marine organisms is according to their **habitat** and movement.

Organisms that live attached to or resting on the sea floor are **benthos**, or benthic life. Corals, sea fans, sea anemones, sea squirts, and some annelids are examples of benthic life. Benthic species are further

classified according to their feeding methods. For example, **bivalve** mollusks, such as oysters, feed by filtering food from the water. Organisms that obtain food in this way are called filter feeders (because, in essence, they "filter" the water). Other forms of benthic life feed on detritus (the remains of plants and animals) that they find along the sea floor.

Plankton

Organisms that move by drifting with the waves and currents are called **plankton**. Plankton are classified as **phytoplankton**

and **zooplankton**. Phytoplankton include diatoms and dinoflagellates that drift in the upper layers of the water, where they carry out **photosynthesis.** Zooplankton feed on phytoplankton. They include small organisms such as the free-swimming **larvae** of benthic species. They also include the adults of other species that are too small to oppose the movement of the water. Zooplankton contain representatives of all marine animals, including fishes in the first stages of development. Among these organisms, however, **krill** are particularly important. Krill are shrimps

1. All marine organisms can be classified into four groups—benthos, plankton, nekton, and neuston. Organisms are placed in these groups according to where they live and how they move. Benthos usually live on the sea floor, either fixed to a surface or moving freely along the floor. Plankton float at various depths. Nekton can swim. Neuston swim on the water's surface. Animals such as sea otters, turtles, and sea birds are considered neuston when they float on the surface, and nekton when they swim under water.

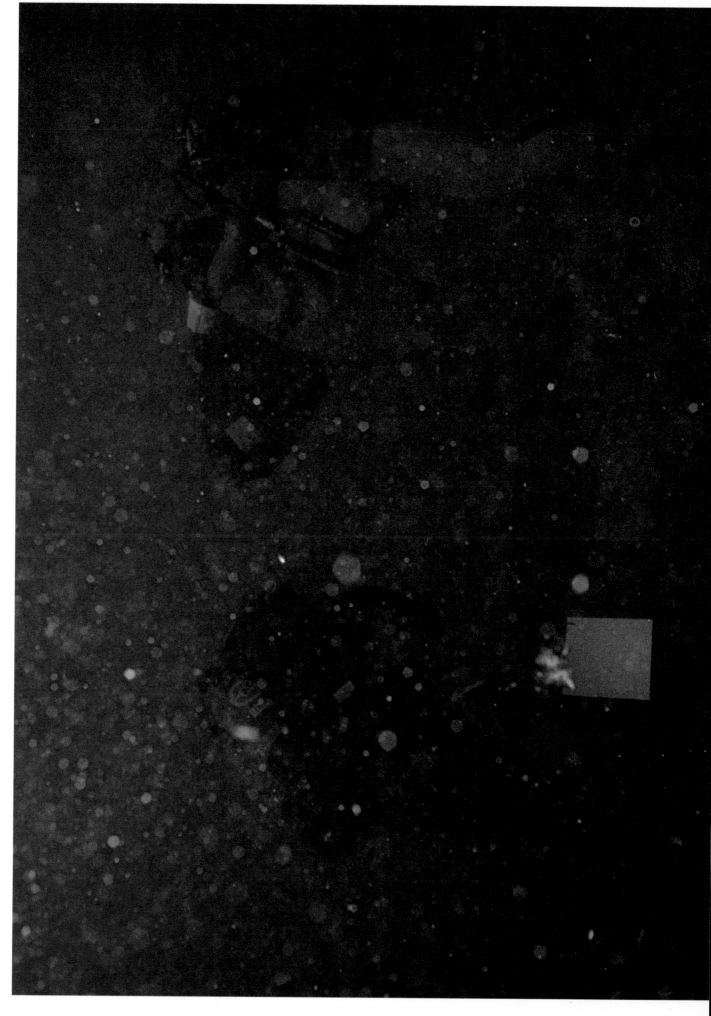

2. A strange effect produced by a flash gun underwater—the light is reflected by planktonic organisms that would otherwise be invisible.

of the *Euphausia* genus. They can be up to 7 centimeters (2.7 in) long and are an important part of the diets of many whales. Other crustaceans, like the **copepods** and rare marine animals such as the arrow worms, are also important parts of plankton. Ecologists distinguish between plankton that can be caught in a fine mesh net and nanoplankton, organisms that are too small to be collected in this way.

Nekton and Neuston

Organisms that do not permanently live on the ocean floor and also do not drift move in two ways. They either swim freely, like fishes, or they move on the water's surface. The free-swimming organisms are **nekton**. Organisms that move along the water's surface are **neuston**.

In fresh water, neuston include many tiny arthropods that can walk on the water without sinking because of the water's surface tension. In the sea, the movement of the water itself breaks up the surface. As a result, movement along the surface can be used only in rock pools and sheltered areas. Neuston organisms of the open sea are usually large, fish-eating vertebrates such as sea birds, seals, or turtles that float and swim on the surface.

Within the nekton community are organisms that swim at various depths. Some visit the sea floor to feed on benthos and plankton. For example, the fishes of the suborder Clupoidea (sardines, herrings, and anchovies) collect plankton using a kind of net formed by the blades of their gills. Because the finest nets cannot trap most phytoplankton, these fishes feed almost solely on zooplankton. Fish that feed on zooplankton are secondary **consumers**.

1. Plankton are a variety of plant-like and animal-like organisms that drift in the water without being able to control their movements. Plankton are subdivided into phytoplankton and zooplankton. "Phytoplankton" comes from a Greek word meaning "drifting plant." Phytoplankton is composed of microscopic

of 100 meters (328 ft). They are very numerous. In fact, 1 centimeter^3 (.06 in^3) of water may contain hundreds of thousands of organisms.

Zooplankton is a varied group of animal-like organisms. They range from protozoa to cnidarians and the larvae of crustaceans and fish. These animals range in size

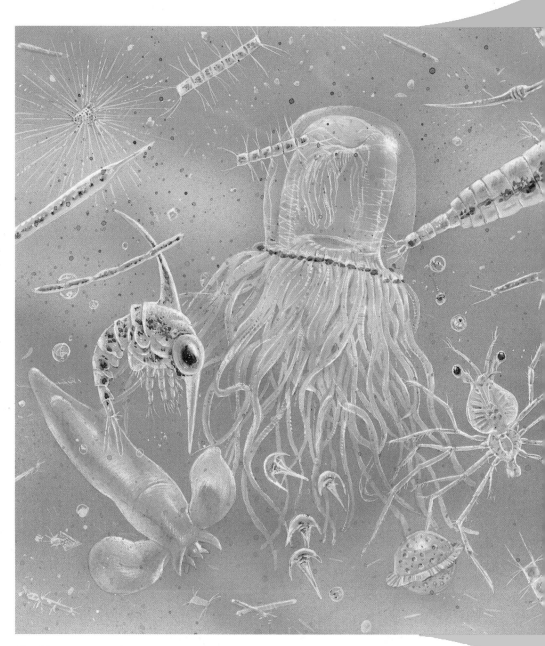

Plankton

single-celled algae, filaments, and tiny protozoa that carry out photosynthesis. These organisms use the energy of sunlight to construct the complex molecules of their tissues from simple chemical substances in the water. Because they depend on light, these organisms live in the upper layers of the ocean to a depth

from a few microns (thousandths of a millimeter) to several centimeters. The zooplankton live together with the phytoplankton.

2. A view of a Mediterranean sea floor with nekton (fish) and benthos (sea fans and algae).

Nekton

Benthos

1

THE FOOD PYRAMID OF THE CONTINENTAL SHELF

Light and Nutrition

As we have already established, the part of the sea where sunlight penetrates is called the photic zone. This area, in which marine animals and people using suitable breathing gear can move like suspended explorers, is the same as the part of the marine environment called the continental shelf. The continental shelf is a transitional zone between dry land and the ocean. In this band of recently submerged land, you can see the effects of agents of erosion such as rivers, glaciers, wind, and rain.

In the photic zone, marine communities are rich and complex. In addition to sunlight, organic and mineral nutrients are plentiful in this area. The nutrients are carried there by rivers and encourage the growth of the algae that serve as food for the higher levels of the **food pyramid**.

Between the beach and the open sea is a sequence of zones. First there is the **intertidal zone**. The intertidal zone stretches from the high tide to the low tide marks. Next is the **neritic zone.** The neritic zone extends from the intertidal zone to the end of the continental shelf. The last zone is the **oceanic zone.** Also called the open ocean, it is inhabited by organisms that are not capable of photosynthesis. Thus, these organisms must feed on organic matter that drifts down from the waters of the continental shelf.

Planktonic Predators

One of the most surprising things about the lowest level of the food pyramid of the continental shelf is the difference between the phytoplankton and the zooplankton that feeds on it. One would expect about ten times more phytoplankton than zooplankton. However, the phytoplankton is equal to about 50 to 70% of the quantity of zooplankton.

This mystery is explained when you look at the life cycles of the two parts— phytoplankton have an average span of about one week per generation. The life span of zooplankton is much slower. Thus, the small animals making up zooplankton can feed on the many generations of phytoplankton that are produced and consumed rapidly.

The food pyramid of the oceans. At the base of the pyramid is the phytoplankton. Phytoplankton include microscopic single-celled organisms such as the yellow-brown algae (**1**) Atlantic coccolithophore, *Emiliana huxleyii*. This algae has a beautiful pierced structure. A number of blue-green algae and diatoms, such as the circular *Arachnoidiscus ehrenbergii* (**2**), of the Pacific. The triangular, shield-shaped *Triceratium favus* is found in all the seas. *Thalassiosina* (**4**), from the Atlantic, is a long chain made up of many small discs. Dinoflagellate protozoans, such as *Gonyaulax tamarensis,*(**5**) of the Pacific, carry out photosynthesis.
Phytoplankton is consumed by drifting zooplankton. Zooplankton are made up of microscopic protozoans such as the foraminifers (**6**) the radiolarians (**7**), jellyfishes, mollusks, and the larvae of crustaceans. Some crustaceans, such as the scampi, *Nephropus norvegicus* (**8**), have amazing structures like miniature monsters and the copepods, such as (**9**) *Calocalanus pavo.*
Above the zooplankton is the vast group of zooplankton–consuming fish such as sardines and

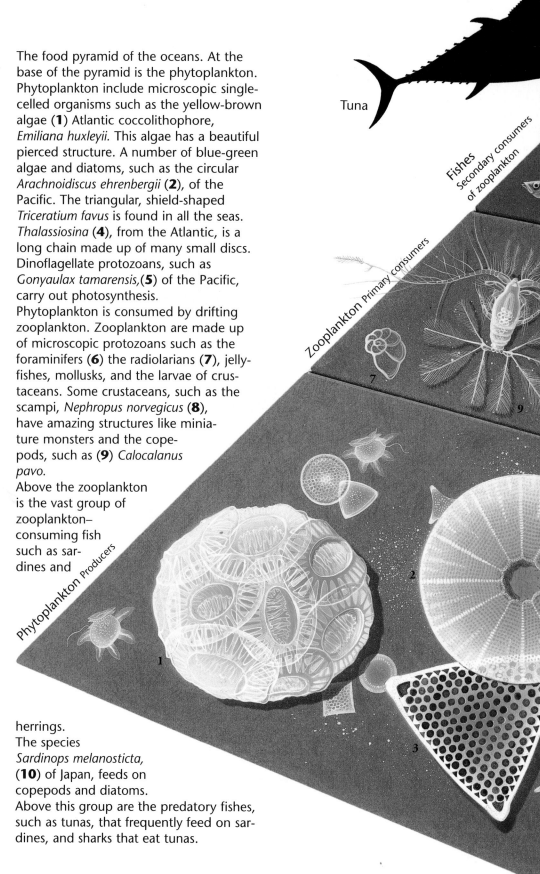

Tuna

Fishes
Secondary consumers of zooplankton

Zooplankton Primary consumers

Phytoplankton Producers

herrings.
The species *Sardinops melanosticta,* (**10**) of Japan, feeds on copepods and diatoms.
Above this group are the predatory fishes, such as tunas, that frequently feed on sardines, and sharks that eat tunas.

Super-predatory fishes

Predatory fishes

Shark

10

8

6

4

5

21

Zooplankton forms the staple diet of many swimming animals, from small crustaceans and fishes to huge whales. There are, however, organisms within the plankton itself that are eager predators of larvae, copepods, and crustaceans. These predators are the spindle-shaped **chaetognaths** and the elegant ctenophores, which are transparent and hard to see even for their prey.

Menacing Burrowers

Among the many lifestyles of the benthic organisms that live in the neritic zone, the most interesting are the burrowers and borers. These animals can make a hole in almost any type of rock to create a permanent refuge.

Many mollusks and annelid worms burrow into soft substrate. There are also borers that can attack wood, the shells of mollusks, and even rock. For example, the eastern chitons (*Lithophaga lithophaga*) dig perfect tunnels into rock using an acidic secretion. Their holes are often visible in shallow waters. They can also be seen on the columns of the Temple of Serapide (Pozzuoli, Italy), the lower part of which was submerged in the sea for a long time.

Among the perforators of mollusks are sponges (cliona), an acorn **barnacle**, and a gastropod mollusk of the genus *Natica*. All these animals can infest and destroy oyster and mussel beds. The best-known wood borers are the ship worms (*Teredo navalis*), which can dig twisted mazes of tunnels into any wooden construction, eventually causing its collapse.

In 1730, ship worms caused great damage to many wooden bulkheads in the Dutch sea defenses. A century earlier, ship worms may have changed the course of European history by infesting the hulls of Philip II's invincible armada when it was moored in Lisbon. The ships were weakened so much they were crushed by a storm that surprised the fleet in the North Sea.

1. After having burrowed into submerged wood, the larvae of the ship worm (*Teredo navalis*) complete their metamorphosis. These lamellibranch mollusks have two tiny valves that they use to dig tunnels in submerged wood. The damage caused is comparable to that caused by termites on land. Ship worms feed on organic particles, filtering them from the water through a siphon.

2. Eastern chitons (*Lithophaga lithophaga*), lamellibranchs similar to common mussels, chemically attack calcium-containing rocks, creating homes in which they live all their life.

3. A grazing leatherjacket (*Odonus niger*); a herbivorous species.

THE GREAT UNDERWATER PRAIRIES

Algae Forests

An area of dense vegetation begins at the upper edge of the continental shelf. This vegetation is made up of algae that form vast underwater prairies. The algal garden can be identified easily from above because it is darker in color than the sea floor. The best-known algae are the species in the *Laminaria* genus. These attach themselves to rocks or pebbles and form living barriers around the coasts. The barriers protect coastal regions from the direct impact of waves. Such protection is so useful that people have transplanted algal barriers into certain areas.

The prairie-forests of *Laminaria* form an interesting habitat for many animals. These include small bryozoans and hydrozoans that establish themselves on the algal leaves, covering them with delicate embroideries. Algae-eating sea urchins (*Echinus* spp. ["spp." is the abbreviation of the plural form of "species;" "sp." is the singular], *Strongylocentrotus* spp.) and brightly colored nudibranch mollusks that feed on algae and hydrozoans are also present.

Underwater Prairies of Flowering Plants

At slightly deeper levels—down to around 50 meters (164 ft)—are prairie-forests of ribbon-like plants. These plants may be up to 1.5 meters (4.9 ft) long, but no more than 1 centimeter (0.39 in) wide. They are a brilliant bright green color and look like algae. However, they are

actually flowering plants. They are the **neptunegrass** (*Posidonia*) of the Mediterranean and the southern coasts of Australia, and the eelgrass (*Zosteraceae*) found in all temperate seas. The flowers of these plants develop at the base of the leaves as small spikes. The pollen has the same weight as sea water. When pollen is released, it floats freely until, with a high degree of probability, it comes to rest on a female flower.

Neptunegrass prairies are rich in unusual plants and animals. The life forms include algae (*Ulvaceae* spp., *Fossiella* spp.), gastropod mollusks, bryozoans, hydrozoans, sea stars, sea cucumbers, bivalve mollusks, and tube worms. There are also many species of *Cypraecea*, mostly tropical mollusks with a porcelain-like shell that is sought-after by collectors. Squid, hermit crabs, sea anemones, and crustaceans are also present.

Unusual Fishes

The fishes from this environment are also very characteristic. Some notable groups are the brightly colored wrasses (Labridae), the sea horses, the pipe fish, the parrotfish, the eels, and species of the genus *Maena*.

The most unusual fishes of the neptunegrass prairies are the sea horses (*Hippocampus* spp.). They differ greatly from the cigar-shaped fishes. With their horse's head, tubular nose, and long, prehensile tail used for anchoring to under-

1. The brown alga *Laminaria digitata* drying out at low tide. These algae are so firmly attached to rocks that severe storms often wash them ashore with large pieces of rock still fixed to their bases. **2.** A closeup of the brown alga *Fucus spiralis* with its characteristic air bladders, which allow it to float. **3.** *Eucus vesiculosus* with its fronds (leaflike structures) spread out in the water thanks to the bladders. These two species prefer the cold North Atlantic coasts of Europe and America. **4.**, **6.** Divers patrolling the underwater prairies of *Posidonia oceanica* off the Egadi Islands, Italy. The neptunegrass flowering plants resemble algae. However, they are capable of more intensive photosynthesis. Up to 7,000 leaves can be found in 1 meter^2 (10.76 ft^2) and are capable of releasing no less than 14 liters (3.6 gal) of oxygen each day, a rate of production around twice that of a temperate forest. Each hectare (2.47 acres) of neptunegrass prairie houses more than 400 plant species and thousands of animal species. **5.** Dry remains of the filaments at the base of neptunegrass (see the illustration on the following page) that the waves have worked into balls and thrown up onto the beach.

2

4

3

5

6

water plants, these small animals swim upright by beating their dorsal fins. The males have a sack in which they carry the eggs laid by the female. In this way the males protect their developing young. Instead of scales, sea horses are covered with bony plates. These plates generally preserve well after the animal dies. Sea horses can occasionally be found intact washed up on the beach. Pipe fish (*Syngnathus acus*) are similar to sea horses, but they swim horizontally, keeping their slim, streamlined bodies stretched out.

Just as odd as the sea horses and pipe fish are the brilliantly colored wrasses. When resting, these fishes lie on their sides looking ill or injured. Specimens of *Labrus tordus* are all female at birth and fairly dull in color. In time, if conditions are favorable and the young animals find fertile territories, they will change into males. They will then grow larger and more brightly colored, spending the rest of their lives in this form.

1. *Posidonia oceanica* again with its characteristic flower spikes. The drawings and the photos show a number of species that normally live among its leaves. **2.** A female rainbow wrasse *(Coris julis).* **3.** A male of the same species. **4.** A slender pipefish *(Syngnathus acus)* belonging to the unusual Syngnathidae family, which also includes the sea horses. **5.** *Cyprea* sp., a gastropod mollusk with a beautiful porcelain-like shell. **6.** A sea horse *(Hippocampus* sp.) anchored to a sea fan by its tail. **7.** A species of sea bream *(Pagurus arrosor)* living in symbiosis with certain sea anemones *(Calliactis parasitica)* fixed to the empty shell occupied by the crustacean. The latter is attacking a sea cucumber *(Holothuria tubulosa).* **8.** Black scorpionfish *(Scorpaena porcus),* a stubby fish about 20 centimeters (7.8 in) long. **9.** A *Thalassoma pavo.* **10.** A five-spotted wrasse *(Crenilabrus quinquemaculatus).* **11.** A wrasse *(Labrus tordus).* Like the rainbow wrasse, it can change its sex with accompanying great changes in appearance.

ANIMAL LIFE OF THE ROCKY SEA BEDS

1. Among the echinodermates that live on shallow rocky sea floors are variegated sea urchins such as *Sphaerechinus granularis.*

1

2

2. A huge shoal of small orange fish, *Pseudanthias squamipinnis,* gather on a coralline sea floor. Thanks to the wealth of life that inhabits them and the extraordinary adaptations of some of the species, coral reefs are a very unusual type of rocky sea floor.

A Rich Variety

The most typical animal life of the continental shelf lives near rocky sea beds. Many **ecological niches** are available in these areas because there is plenty of light. As a result there is a great variety of marine animals. The most unusual adaptations are also found among animals in these areas.

In rocky sea beds, the rocks may be covered with calcium-containing algae, sea anemones, acorn barnacles, sea fans, mussels, and other animals and plants that can change the look of the environment. Barriers are created among the rocks. Fissures and cavities are opened. In addition many other kinds of shelters are created to provide a fairly easy life for organisms that can adapt to take advantage of the opportunities presented.

There is no way to mention all the groups in this large community. Thus, we will look only at some of the most common and attractive that live in the Atlantic Ocean and the Mediterranean Sea.

Sea Stars and Sea Urchins

Among the most easily recognizable species are the large sea stars. For example, *Marthasterias glacialis* lives in the Atlantic, the North Sea, and the Mediterranean. It may reach 1 meter (3.2 ft) in diameter and has five arms dotted with spines. Its color varies according to the water depth. In shallow water it is green. In deeper water it is yellow or pink.

Other sea stars, like the beautiful *Crossaster papposus,* found in the North Sea and the Atlantic, or *Ophidiaster ophidianus,* of the southern Mediterranean, are a bright red color. Some species divide into many pieces if subjected to stress. Each piece can then develop into a new individual.

The brittle stars are similar to sea stars. However, the brittle stars have slim arms that move rapidly. They are usually less than 30 centimeters (12 in) in diameter and are dull in color. Like sea stars, brittle stars are predators of mollusks.

Sea urchins live in colonies on the rocks close to the shore. They are much more numerous than the sea stars. Among the most common species found in the Atlantic and the Mediterranean are *Parocentrotus lividus* and *Arbacia lixula.*

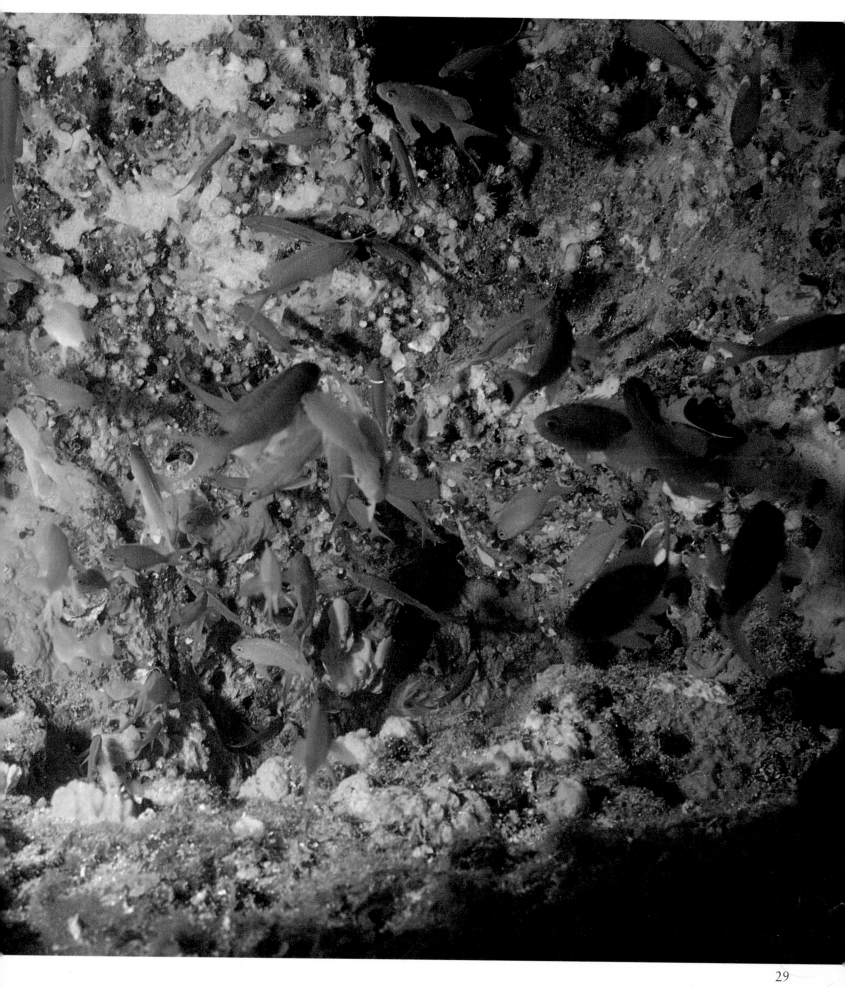

Both species are almost black in color. Another common species is *Sphaerechinus granularis*. It is an attractive violet color and has rounded spines.

Crabs, Shrimps, and Lobsters

Many crustaceans inhabit rocky environments. The crabs, hermit crabs, shrimps, and lobsters are the best known. However, small isopods and parasitic barnacles are also common.

In general, crustaceans feed on small prey. Hermit crabs are crustaceans well known for their ability to reuse empty gastropod mollusk shells. Some hermit crab species have a symbiotic relationship with sea anemones, which they carry on their shells. The stocky crab *Dromia vulgaris* has a similar habit. It often disguises itself by carrying a sponge on its back. This trait has earned it the nickname of the "porter crab."

One of the largest crustaceans is the lobster species *Palinuris vulgaris*. It is often as much as 50 centimeters (20 in) in length. It usually hides itself among the rocks at depths of between 15 and 100 meters (49 and 328 ft). An even bigger species is the blue-mottled European lobster (*Homarus gammarus*) with its two large pincer-like claws. At the opposite end of the range are the palaemon, which are transparent shrimps that look like miniature lobsters. These shrimps are just a few centimeters in length and have long, thread-like feelers.

Murices, Oysters, and Octopuses

Among the many different mollusks—in economic terms among the most important species—are the well-known murices (*Murex*). Murices are gastropods that are edible and were once used to produce a purple dye. Another well-known genus is that of the sea ear (*Haliotis*), with its mother-of-pearl shell perforated with a row of holes.

Bivalve mollusks seems to have more in common with a restaurant menu than the records of a naturalist. Among this group are oysters (*Ostrea edulis*), mussels (*Mytilus edulis*), eastern chitons (*Lithophaga lithophaga*), and scallops (*Pecten jacobaeus*).

The most curious of the rocky environment mollusks is the octopus (*Octopus vulgaris*). The octopus is a large member of the cephalopod class. It may weigh up to 25 kilograms (55 lbs) and have a diameter of up to 3 meters (10 ft) with its eight tentacles spread out. Apart from its dimensions, octopuses are well known for their well-developed eyes, which are similar to those of vertebrates. According to naturalists who have studied them, the octopuses' nervous systems are so well developed, these animals can be trained almost as well as the most intelligent vertebrates.

The Fishes of the Rocky Sea Beds

Fishes are very common and varied in appearance in areas with rocky sea beds. The adaptations best-suited to benthic life are found among the Selachii. The benthic species in this class include small sharks, such as the dogfish, and the rays, which have a flat shape suited to life on the sea bed, generally in sandy areas.

Adaptations similar to those of the rays are also seen among the anglerfish (*Lophius piscatorius*). These species reach up to 2 meters (6.5 ft) in length. Unlike the rays, anglerfish have no electrical organs or poisonous spines. They have huge mouths and three long spines between their eyes that act as bait. The anglerfish lie unmoving on the sea bed at depths of up to 500 meters (1,640 ft). There they patiently wait for fish that approach while looking for food. Another typical predator of the rocky sea beds is the moray eel (*Muraena helena*). These snake-like fishes grow to be as much as 130 cm (51 in) long. They are equipped with powerful jaws and inhabit cracks in the rocks, ready to dart out at the first sign of prey.

Other well-known predators of the rocks are the Serranidae—the family to which the combers, sea bass, groupers, and similar fishes belong. Groupers are husky fish with huge mouths. They lie in wait for their prey at depths ranging from a few dozen to 1,000 meters (3,280 ft).

1. Sea stars are perhaps the most spectacular echinoderms that can commonly be seen in coastal environments. They can be found in all seas from the subarctic regions to the tropics. The species photographed here inhabits the coral reefs of the Red Sea. **2.** A *Carpilius convexus* crab on the Bonaire coral reef in the Netherlands Antilles. The crustaceans are one of the best-known classes of arthropods and, apart from the insects, are also among the most numerous. There are around 25,000 species, most of them aquatic, and some of them able to grow to considerable sizes. They are characterized by antennae on the second and third segments of their bodies

and pincers on the fourth. **3.** A bed of mussels *(Mytilus edulis)* on a rock partially uncovered at low tide in the Ligurian Sea, off the coast of Italy.

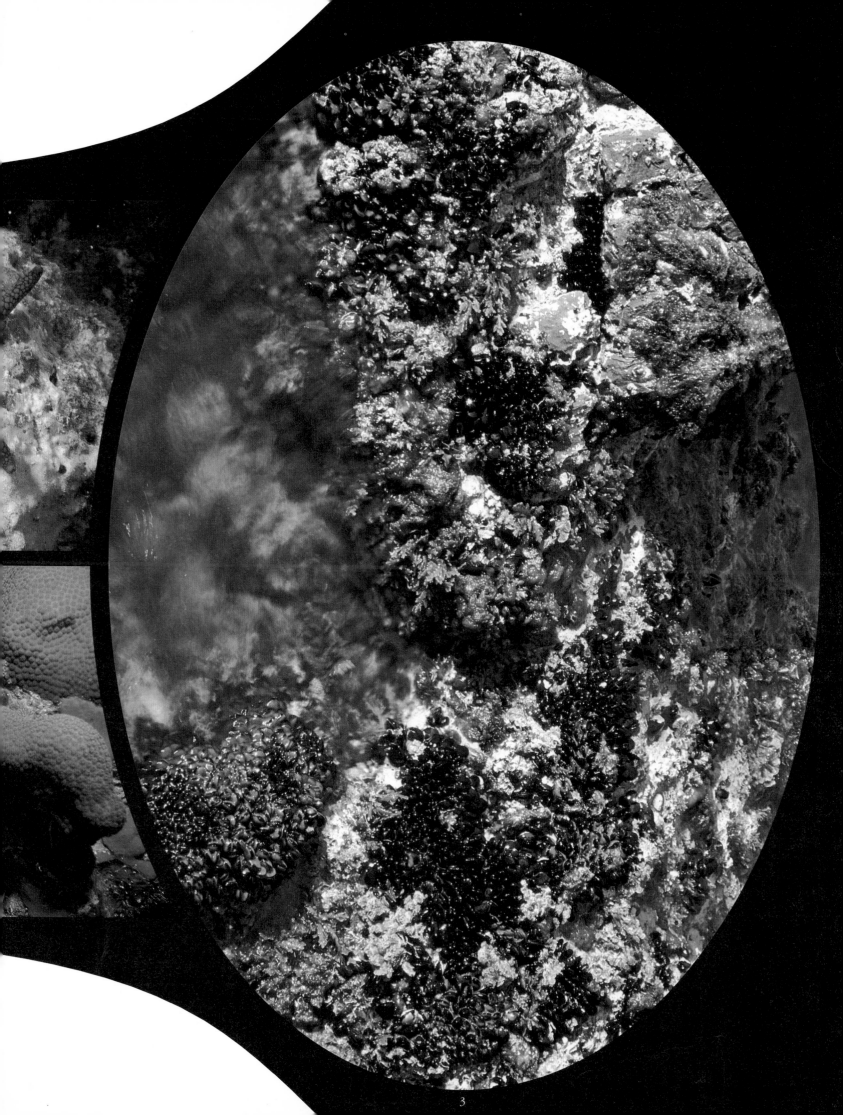

The giant grouper (*Epinephelus guaza*) may reach a length of 1.5 meters (5 ft), while the stone bass (*Polyprion americanus*), found in the eastern Atlantic and the Mediterranean, may reach up to 2 meters (6.5 ft) in length and 50 kilograms (110 lbs) in weight.

An interesting form of **hermaphroditism** exists among the Serranidae and the Labridae. All the young fish—between two and five years of age, depending on the species—mature as females and reproduce as such. Later, at ages between seven and ten years, they change into males. These fishes then continue their reproductive lives as males.

The red mullet (*Mullus surmuletus*), the armored red scorpionfish (*Scorpaena scro-*

Another family that is well-adapted to life in rocky environments is the Sparidae. The fish in the Sparidae family are not bottom-dwellers. They are powerful swimmers that move close to the sea bed at shallow depths. Many well-known and highly prized food fish belong to this family. Examples include the dentex (*Dentex dentex*), the gilthead bream (*Sparus auratus*), species of the genus *Diplodus*, the saddled bream (*Oblata melanura*), the bogue (*Boops boops*), and *Boops salpe*.

This brief review could not be concluded without mentioning the damselfish (*Chromis chromis*). The damselfish is a small brown fish of only a few centimeters in length. It has a characteristic forked tail and can be seen in the waters of Italian

1. An octopus on a rocky sea floor. The mollusks are a diverse phylum of invertebrates. There are 80,000 species that are often very different from one another. All mollusks share a foot and a mantle.

2. In contrast to the silvery bream grazing in the foreground on a rocky sea floor, you can see a brightly colored wrasse emerging from the background.

1

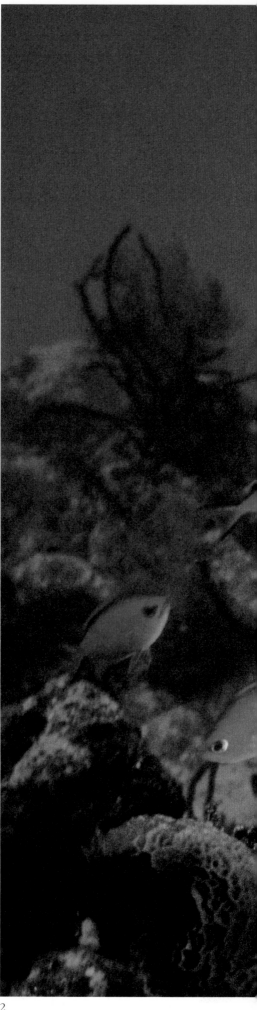

2

fa), the black scorpionfish (*Scorpaena porcus*), and the gurnard (*Triglia lucerna*) are also benthic fishes. Red mullets have a double barb (where their sense of taste is located) and stunning yellow stripes along their sides.

Another family of benthic fishes are the variously colored blennies. These have elongated bodies, blunt and almost vertical faces, a long dorsal fin, and small ventral fins. Blennies hide in holes and small cracks in the rocks, which they manage to slip into easily thanks to a slimy secretion that covers their bodies. The smallest species live in rock pools. The larger ones live in rocky areas at greater depths.

ports. The young of this species are bright blue in color, recalling its tropical origins. The damselfish belongs to a tropical family (Pomacentridae), of which it is the only representative in the Mediterranean.

SANDY AND MUDDY SEA FLOORS

Filtering Burrowers

At first sight, sandy sea floors appear to be less rich in life than the rocky areas. You may think these areas resemble the deserts of dry land. However, this comparison is not valid since there is no lack of water on the sandy sea floor. What is lacking is a substrate on which large organisms can anchor themselves. Other organisms have adapted to the environment by hiding themselves in the sand with only their tentacles, foot, gills, eyes, or mouth emerging.

Among the most numerous animals in sandy sea beds are bivalve mollusks. They burrow into the sand at a slant with their siphons protruding on the surface. The **siphons** are tubular organs with two openings through which the sea water passes and is filtered. One opening is an intake, the other is an outlet.

Many bivalve mollusks from the sandy environments are well known. For example, the species of the *Venus* and *Venerupis* genera are commonly called clams. The shells of clams are covered with stripes that run parallel to the shell's edge. Cockles are similar to clams. They have finely ribbed robust shells. The delicate *Tellina donax* has a pink translucent shell.

Specialist echinoderms like the flattened sea star of the Asteroidea class, brittle stars (*Ophiura texturata*), and some "irregular" sea urchins live on sandy sea beds. They are small and oval in shape. These echinoderms are covered with spines that may be very long.

Among the annelids, or sea worms, are sedentary species that live in slimy mucous or calcium-containing tubes they build themselves. Only their brightly colored gills emerge from the tubes. These gills resemble flowers and are ready to disappear at the slightest disturbance.

Poisonous Fishes and Flat Fishes

The bony fishes that have adapted to sandy environments have evolved the ability to dig. Their eyes shift to the tops of their heads, and their bodies are often flattened. The stargazers (Uranoscopidae) have flattened heads with eyes pointing upward. Their gray-brown coloring is an effective camouflage. Lying still on the sea floor, the little *Uranoscopus scaber* uses a worm-like tentacle beneath its tongue as bait. This species is about 25 cm (9.8 in)

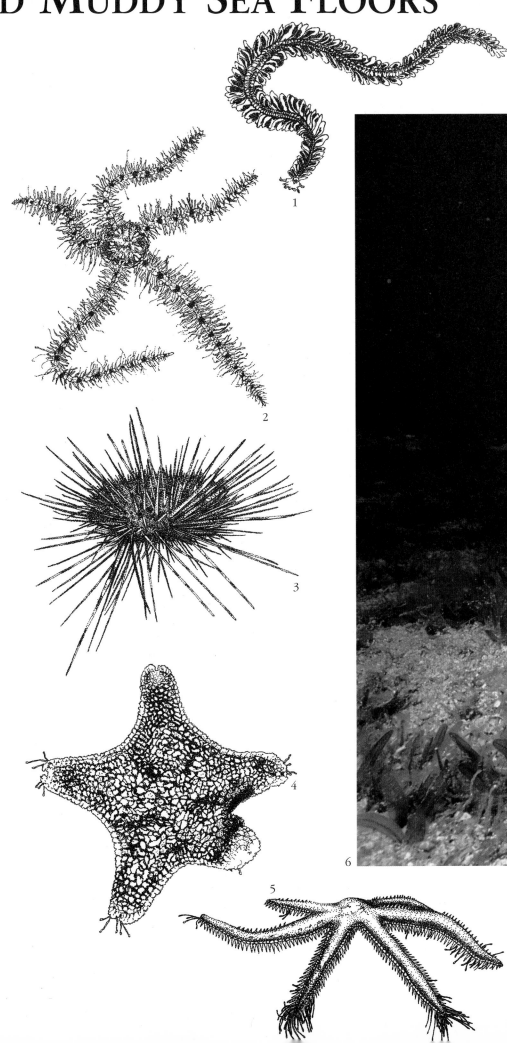

A number of typical inhabitants of sandy and muddy sea floors. **1.** A polychaete (segmented) worm of the Errantia subclass—the paddle worm *(Phyllodoce paretti).* **2.** An echinoderm, the brittle-star *(Ophiotrix fragilis).* **3.** An echinoid, *Centrostephanus longispinus.* **4. 5.** Two sea stars, *Asterina gibbosa* and *Luidia ciliaris.* **6.** A bivalve

mollusk, the pen shell *(Pinna nobilis).* **7.** An anthozoan, the sea anemone *(Cerianthus membranaceus).* **8.** A sedentary polychaete, *Spirographis spallanzanii.* Three bivalve mollusks—**9.** a cockle *(Rudicardium turbercula-tum),* **10.** a clam *(Donax trunculus),* and **11.** a razor shell *(Ensis siliqua).*

long. In case of danger, it quickly digs a refuge in gravel or sand using its pectoral and ventral fins. If necessary, it can also use electrical organs located behind its eyes or injure an enemy with three poisonous spines, located on its gill cover.

The weaverfish (Trachinidae family) are similar to the stargazers. They also have three poisonous spines, located on the first dorsal fin. The body of these fishes is long and flat. The mouth opening is strongly tilted, and the eyes are located high up on the head. When lying buried in the sand, only the eyes and first dorsal fin emerge. The fish is then perfectly hidden from both predators and potential prey.

Flat fishes in the Pleuronectiformes order can also hide easily in the sand. This order includes sole, turbot, and plaice. These fishes have evolved in an unusual way. Their eyes and the pigmented part of their back have moved to one side of the body. It is as if they have laid down on the sea floor on one side and have adapted to this position. Their strange evolutionary history can be seen in the development of their young. The young are born symmetrical, then they undergo a major transformation. At a certain age, one of the two eyes migrates until it is located near the other. At this point the young fish lays on the sea floor on the blind side of its body, adopting the position in which it will remain all its life.

The cartilaginous fishes include sharks, rays, skates, and torpedo fish. The rays and skates have flat bodies and live mainly on sandy or muddy sea floors. Here, they bury themselves to a depth of a few centimeters. Both rays and the sharks are oviparous. They lay large eggs in rectangular horny shells on the sea floor.

1. You may have some unexpected encounters on sandy and muddy sea floors. Here the photographer has surprised a fast-moving lobster (*Palinurus vulgaris*), a typical inhabitant of rocky sea floors. **2.** A "Panaeus" shrimp (*Panaeus kerathurus*), up to 20 centimeters (7.8 in) in length. It is found on the sandy sea floors of the Mediterranean and the Atlantic. **3.** A guardian shrimp (*Pontonia custos*), an animal of just 3 centimeters (1.1 in) in length. It lives on the sandy sea floors or among the neptunegrass prairies of the Mediterranean. It normally lives within the large *Pinna noblis.* **4.** Mantis shrimp (*Squilla mantis*), a stomatopod crustcean that grows up to 25 centimeters (9.8 in) in length. **5.** The spider crab (*Maja squinado*) is a large, well-armed crab. **6.** A sea bream (*Pagellus erythrinus*), a sparid (family Sparidae) of modest size— 25 centimeters (9.8 in)—but with large eyes. **7.** A stingray (*Dasyatis pastinaca*). This ray has a poisonous spine on its tail.

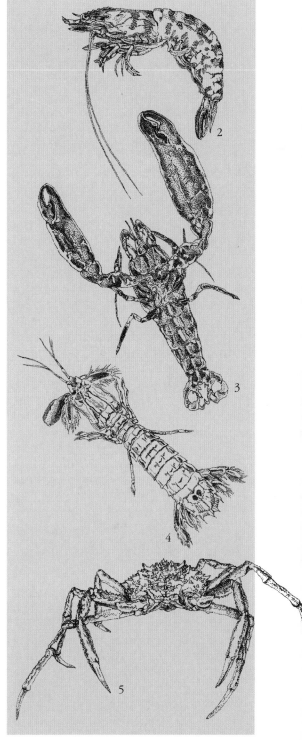

1

2

3

4

5

6

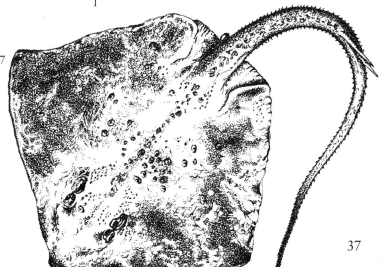

7

37

THE OPEN SEA

Jellyfishes

Beyond the coastal waters and over the deepest part of the continental shelf is a huge floating world that is independent of the sea floor. This is the **pelagic** environment. The pelagic world is the largest of the Earth's ecosystems. It is rich in plankton and nekton. The nekton is composed mainly of fishes that can swim long distances at high speeds.

The pelagic ecosystem is supported by the growth of phytoplankton. This growth is made possible by photosynthesis and by the presence of nitrogen and phosphorus carried into the sea by rivers. The phytoplankton is consumed by the zooplankton. In turn the zooplankton is consumed by vast numbers of plankton and nekton species.

Among the best-known predatory plankton species are the jellyfishes. They are a common sight in seas worldwide. In contrast to their transparent and delicate bodies, these animals have fearsome offensive weapons. Their tentacles carry many special capsules called nematocysts. The nematocysts can cause severe stings when they touch other organisms. The sea wasps (*Chironex fleckeri*) of the Indo-Pacific are so dangerous that their stings can kill a human within 3-20 minutes. At least 50 fatal attacks have been reported along the Australian coast.

Sharks

The sharks are a well-known group of pelagic fishes. There are about 250 species. They are subdivided into about twenty families. All sharks are predatory and have streamlined bodies that allow them to swim very rapidly.

The great swimming ability of sharks is important for two reasons. First, sharks have no swim bladder and therefore cannot remain suspended in the water unless they keep moving. Second, most sharks do not have the special muscles that keep a current of water flowing over a fish's gills. In most sharks, this current is provided by the animal's movement through the water. Therefore, if a shark is caught in a net, it will usually die through oxygen deprivation.

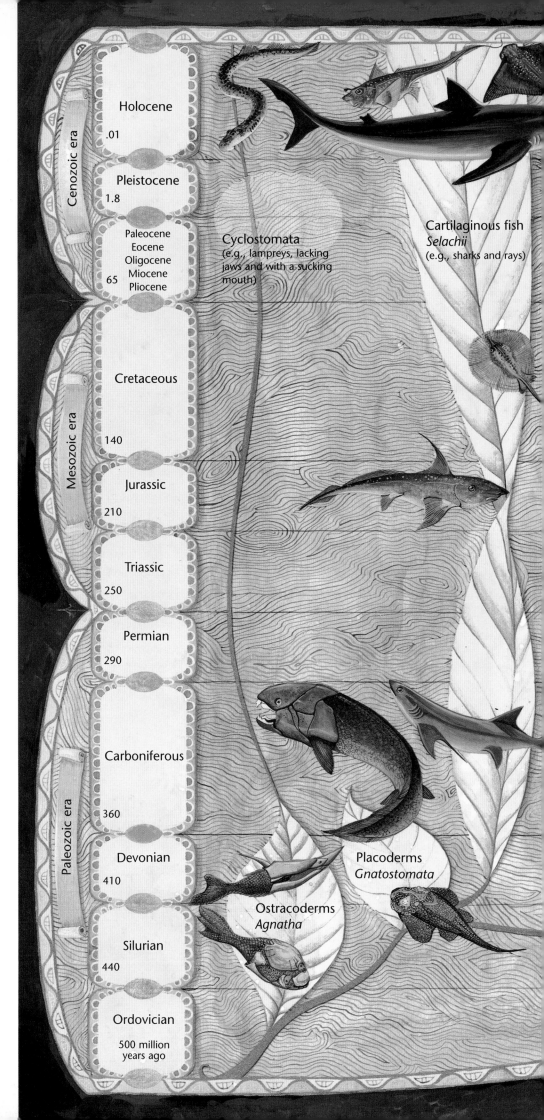

Cartilaginous fish
Selachii
(e.g., sharks and rays)

Cyclostomata
(e.g., lampreys, lacking jaws and with a sucking mouth)

Placoderms
Gnatostomata

Ostracoderms
Agnatha

Cenozoic era	Holocene .01
	Pleistocene 1.8
	Paleocene Eocene Oligocene Miocene Pliocene 65
Mesozoic era	Cretaceous 140
	Jurassic 210
	Triassic 250
Paleozoic era	Permian 290
	Carboniferous 360
	Devonian 410
	Silurian 440
	Ordovician 500 million years ago

Bony fish
Teleostei
Attinopterygii
The group comprising
the most species
(e.g., tuna)

Bony fish
Holostei
Attinopterygii
(e.g., bowfin,
Amia calva)

Bony fish
Chondrostei
Actinopterygii
live in cold deep
water (e.g., sturgeon)

Acanthodii

Bony fish
Sarcopterygii
A small group of fishes
that live in warm and
fresh water and are
able to breathe air.
The amphibians derive
from this group
(e.g.,*Latimeria*)

Fishes are not
a homogeneous
class of animals.
They are an
assembly of classes
that share only the fact
that they are aquatic
vertebrates with gills. The
existing fish belong to three
different classes—Cyclostomata, those
that lack jaws; Agnatha, (like the
extinct ostracoderms) which are
the cartilaginous fishes and the
bony fishes equipped with
jaws; and Gnatostomata,
like the extinct
placoderms.

Not all sharks are dangerous. Many species, like the dogfish (*Scyliorhinus canicula*) and the smooth hound (*Mustelus mustelus*), are small and relatively harmless. Others, like the basking shark (*Cetorhinus maximus*), have highly specialized habits. These sharks may reach as much as 13 meters (43 ft) in length and weigh up to 7,250 kilograms (16,000 lbs). Amazingly, the basking shark feeds only on plankton. There are, however, dangerous predators such as the great white shark, which may grow up to 12 meters (40 ft) in length and, when given the opportunity, will attack humans.

Migrators Large and Small
Among the bony fishes, the most typical inhabitants of the open sea are tunas, mackerels, pilchards, anchovies, and herrings. Most of these fishes travel in schools. Periodically, the schools migrate from their usual feeding grounds to the areas where they reproduce. The most dramatic migrations are those of the tunas (*Thunnus thynnus*). These fishes spend the winters in the Atlantic Ocean and migrate to the Mediterranean Sea to reproduce. A related species, the albacore (*Thunnus alalunga*) reproduces in the Atlantic near the Canaries, the Azores, Madeira, and in the Pacific near Midway Island. The Atlantic populations then migrate north as far as Ireland. Those of the Pacific head to the seas of Alaska. Other Pacific populations migrate instead from east to west, swimming between California and Japan.

The tunas reach the Mediterranean in April, after having spent the winter in the Atlantic feeding on herrings, sardines, mackerels, and other fishes. The sexually mature examples are at least three years old. These mature fishes measure 1 meter (3.3 ft) in length and weigh 15 kilograms (33 lbs). They continue to grow throughout their lives. By the time they are 13 years old, they may be more than 2.5 meters (8.2 ft) long and weigh around 400 kilograms (880 lbs). In the mid-Atlantic, many solitary and very old examples have been captured. These fishes were as much as 5 meters (16 ft) in length and weighed no less than 1,600 kilograms (3,527 lbs).

Tunas swim close to the surface in the Mediterranean. They follow a route parallel to the coast in water between 16 and 19°C (60 and 66°F). They head toward their reproduction areas located around the Balearic Islands and in the triangle between Sicily, Sardinia, and Tunisia, where they lay their eggs in June. People have developed special techniques for capturing these huge fishes. However, those that escape the nets will return to the

Atlantic, covering many thousands of kilometers in just a few months.

Another much smaller migratory fish is the mackerel (*Scomber scombrus*). This fish belongs to the same family as the tuna and the albacore. It is common in temperate and cold regions on both sides of the Atlantic and in the Mediterranean. There is a similar species in Japan (*Scomber japonicus*) that prefers slightly warmer water.

The mackerel occupies a key position in the food chain of pelagic fishes. Mackerels

consume a great amount of zooplankton, making it available to the larger fishes and also to humans in a form suited to their feeding habits. Mackerels reproduce in spring along the Atlantic and Mediterranean

1. A giant manta *(Manta birostris)*, a raji-form belonging to the Mobulidae family that includes unusual rays that have abandoned life on the sea floor and adapted to feeding on plankton. They are found in

polyps. In autumn and winter, the polyps divide to create jellyfishes. **3.** A vortex of carangids *(Caranx* sp.) in a dense school in the waters off Borneo. The highly coordinated directional movement is typical of

3

coasts. Each female lays about 500,000 eggs, each about 1 millimeter (0.003 in) in diameter. Following the reproductive season, the adults stop feeding on plankton and begin to eat other fishes, especially sardines and anchovies. In this way, they

the warm temperate and tropical seas. This example was photographed off the Maldives. **2.** A jellyfish *(Pelagia noctiluca).* The eggs of the jellyfish hatch into larvae that soon settle and develop into solitary

these schools. Schooling reduces the pressure of predators through their organization.

create a sufficient store of fat to survive the cold winter. Early in the autumn, they leave the coastal waters and head to the North Sea, where they descend to great depths and spend the winter, without eating, in a kind of hibernation in the cold and dark.

Herrings (*Clupea harengus*) also complete notable migrations to reproduce. They are typical representatives of the Clupeidae family and migrate to ensure that they always remain in water with a temperature between 6 and 15°C (43 and 59°F). At these temperatures, their floating eggs hatch in just over one week and therefore do not remain exposed to plankton-eaters for too long. Among these plankton-eaters are the herrings themselves. Like mackerels, they form an important link in the food chain of the pelagic organisms. Other well-known members of the Clupeidae family that swim in great schools in warm waters are sardines and anchovies.

This illustration depicts an imaginary, but theoretically possible, event in a corner of the ocean during the Tertiary Period, 5 million years ago. A school of killer whales 6 to 8 meters (20 to 26 ft) long are attacking a giant shark with huge teeth (*Carcharodon megalodon*). The shark is 20 meters (66 ft) long and weighs 30 tons. There is no evidence that such attacks actually took place, but we know that killer whales do not hesitate to attack other whales, and that these cetaceans certainly existed 5 million years ago. The giant shark certainly fed on large prey, including perhaps various cetaceans. Some of these, such as killer whales, were sufficiently equipped to repel the attacks of the shark and perhaps attack in return. Very probably we will never know whether this illustration is pure fantasy or whether it is an accurate reconstruction of a lost world.

THE OCEAN DEPTHS

The Detritus Chain

Beyond the edge of the continental shelf, the sea floor falls away very sharply in the relatively short and steep section called the continental slope. The continental slope is between a few hundred and just under 4,000 meters (13,123 ft) deep. At this point the slope begins to flatten out but continues to descend until it reaches the abyssal plain at around 5,000 meters (16, 404 ft).

At these depths there is no possibility of plant life, and therefore the abyssal ecosystem is incomplete. The organisms living there feed on the detritus of organic material that sinks down from the upper levels, or they are predators. Among the consumers of detritus are a number of tube worms, brittle stars, sea cucumbers, sponges, crustaceans, and the scaphopod mollusks with their unusual shells shaped like tiny elephant's tusks. Most of these organisms have a much higher than average water content. For example, the sea cucumbers are 97% water. They are thus able to stay alive using a small amount of

energy. They are also of low food value to predators.

Spiders and Dragons of the Depths

Predators includes brittle stars, the abyssal fishes, giant squids, and many specialized animals such as the sea spiders. The sea spiders belong to the Pycnogonidae class of marine chelicerates. They have a pair of chelifores similar to the chelicerae of land spiders.

Most sea spiders are very small—only 1 to 10 millimeters (0.039 to 0.39 in) in length. They are consumers of detritus. Certain abyssal species, like *Colossendeis colossea,* have a body longer than 5 centimeters (1.9 in) and a leg span of almost 60 centimeters (24 in). They prey on hydroids, corals, sea anemones, bryozoans, and sponges. Sea spiders use their chelifores to tear prey and carry the pieces to their mouths.

All the abyssal fishes are predators. They have enormous mouths, frequently equipped with needle-sharp teeth, which they use to hang onto their prey. The

shapes of these animals are amazingly bizarre. They often have long or flattened bodies with their eyes on the tops of their heads. They may also have long appendages extending from their fins or their upper or lower jaws. Many produce light by using specialized organs called **photophores**, which are located in various parts of their bodies. Among the ways in which this light is used, one of the most notable is as bait. The light is given off at the end of an appendage like a living fishing rod. It attracts the small fishes and crustaceans that normally feed on plankton that also produce light.

The Legend of the Kraak

For thousands of years, the ocean depths have featured in legends about large and terrible monsters. The frightening Kraak, which was dreaded by Dutch navigators, was a huge octopus that could capture and sink a ship. A similar monster was described by Jules Verne in his adventure story *Twenty Thousand Leagues Under the Sea.*

For a long time, the existence of gigantic cephalapods was unproven. All the stories were a mixture of legend and science fiction. Then, increasingly frequent reports from whalers spoke of huge squid arms found in the stomachs of sperm whales. Research completed in the late nineteenth century unexpectedly demonstrated that giant squids (*Architeuthis*) live thousands of meters below the surface of the oceans. These squids have eight arms, generally around 4 to 6 meters (13 to 20 ft) in length, and two longer tentacles that may reach up to 17 meters (56 ft). The largest example ever caught (at Thimble Tickle, Newfoundland, in 1878) measured around 20 meters (66 ft) in length, of which no less than 12 meters (40 ft) were accounted for by the mantle, head, and shorter arms!

These huge animals are the favorite food of sperm whales. Sperm whales have teeth rather than the baleen filter of whales that eat plankton. To feed, sperm whales dive thousands of meters. Then they engage in great struggles with the giant squids. These fights often leave the whales with scars. Although giant squids cannot really sink ships or even boats (they never even come to the surface unless they are dying), they certainly resemble people's worst nightmares.

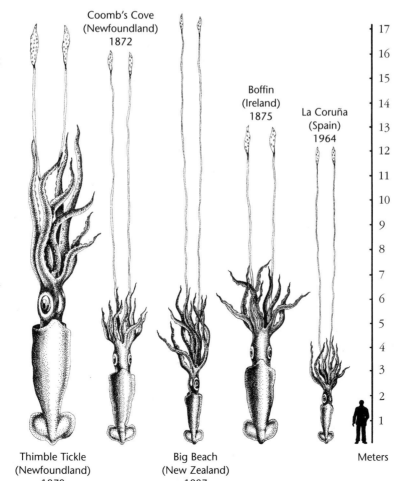

The largest examples of giant squid ever caught compared with a human.

On the facing page: A number of unusual deep-sea fishes.

1. The cestoid *Regaleceus glesne.*

2. A school of *Sternoptyx diaphana.*

3. *Linophryne arborifer* equipped with a luminous feeler and an enormous toothed mouth.

4. *Saccopharynx ampullaceus.*

5. *Melanocetus johnsoni.*

6. *Eupharynx pelecanoides,* all with enormous mouths.

Coomb's Cove (Newfoundland) 1872

Boffin (Ireland) 1875

La Coruña (Spain) 1964

Thimble Tickle (Newfoundland) 1878

Big Beach (New Zealand) 1887

Meters

17 16 15 14 13 12 11 10 9 8 7 6 5 4 3 2 1

EXPLOITATION OF THE SEA

Nature's Last Stronghold

In contrast with continental environments, the marine environments have remained more or less intact. They are in the same condition as they were tens of thousands of years ago. The farming of fishes or crustaceans for food uses advanced technology. However, it is still a minor activity. The food resources offered by the sea are still generally able to withstand modern methods of hunting and gathering.

Modern fishing techniques are not comparable to those of the past. Fishing boats are larger and are fitted with more efficient engines and equipment for locating schools of fish. They are also fitted with

A reconstruction of a jetty at the end of Cannery Row, a famous street in the port of Monterey, California. Here, an equally famous factory canned sardines in the '30s and '40s. In that era, the Hovden Canning Company processed huge quantities of sardines each day. The fish were unloaded from the boats in a chaos of grating noise, stinks, and poetry, as John Steinbeck wrote in his 1945 novel, *Cannery Row* (and later in its light-hearted sequel, *Sweet Thursday*). Steinbeck was often found on this remarkable street (and was portrayed there by the painter Bruce Ariss asleep aboard an old Packard). Alongside the sardine canneries was the home of Ed Ricketts' Pacific Biological Laboratories. Ricketts was a brilliant naturalist. He collected and studied examples of marine animals from Monterey Bay. He was also a great friend of Steinbeck's, his admirer and patron and who used him as a model for one of the main characters ("Doc") in the two aforementioned novels. He and Steinbeck also did one book together, *The Sea of Cortez*, which chronicled a field trip that the two men took together, with Steinbeck handling the "color" content of the record, while Ricketts penned the scientific aspects. Ricketts died in 1948, run down by a train. With him died his remarkable laboratory, and the sardine cannery closed during the same period.

systems for processing and preserving the catch. Moreover, the demand for fishes by a rapidly expanding human population is increasingly heavy. Thus, the traditional species are hunted even more intensively, while new species that previously had no commercial value are being caught as well.

Over-fishing

The research carried out since the turn of the 20th century has shown that there are limits to the possible exploitation of the great schools of fish. Beyond these limits, if people increase their fishing activities, the catches will actually fall instead of rise. This concept can be best explained with a practical example.

1. With an annual catch of 30% (six young fish from every 20), a fish population can be maintained, and older and larger examples can be exploited (four fish from every 14 the second year, three from ten the third year and two from seven the fourth year). **2.** If the annual catch is increased to 90% of the total population, the resource will be destroyed within the second year. The larger fish will disappear from the remaining population and from among those that have been caught.

Imagine that a fleet of fishing boats catches a certain percentage of individuals (for example sardines, herrings, or tunas) from a particular fish population each year. In 50 days of fishing, the boats catch 50 tons of fish. In 100 days, they catch 80 tons. At first look, it seems that the longer the boats fish, the more fish they will catch, even though the total is proportionally lower. In reality, by continuing to fish for the longer period, the fish being caught will be much smaller and the total weight of the catch will be reduced within a few years.

In the first case, the boats might catch a few large fish. In the second case—in spite

of the longer period of fishing—the 80 tons of fish will be composed of a larger number of smaller individuals.

There are even more extreme situations. For example, after seven years of no fishing in the North Sea because of World War II (1939-1945), the average size of the fish being caught increased. In addition, more fish were caught.

It is not in the best interests of people to exploit marine resources irrationally. However, it tends to happen because of the problems of common property. In the collective exploitation of a resource, an individual may cheat by taking a larger share than is due. That individual will gain an economic advantage. However, the community as a whole suffers. The exploitation of marine resources therefore needs careful planning and careful control over the harvesting.

One of the most extreme examples of over-exploitation is that of the Pacific sardine (*Sardinops caerulea*). This species was once found in enormous schools along the coasts of North America from Alaska to Baja California. The exploitation of the species began early in this century. It rapidly expanded until 1936 and 1937. As the amounts caught (800,000 tons in the best years) exceeded the demand, the remaining sardines were used as animal feed and to make fertilizers.

However, the size of the catch began to decline rapidly until the sardine industry collapsed disastrously in the early 1950s.

A contrasting example is that of the halibut (*Hippoglossus hippoglossus*). This Nordic giant of flat fishes reaches up to 3 meters (9.8 ft) in length and may weigh up to 600 kilograms (1,322 lbs). From 1915 to 1927, the Canadian and United States halibut catch declined by 60 to 70%. The two governments decided to intervene with strict and efficient regulations. Today the annual catch is limited to 30,000 to 50,000 tons to prevent over-exploitation of the resource.

3. Off Cape Bòn, in Tunisia, a group of fishermen with the boats arranged in a circle. They are slowly raising the nets of the "death chamber," in which a number of tunas have been caught. **5.** The operation is now almost completed and the blue Mediterranean waters are boiling with the vainly struggling fish. **4.** A closeup of the nets piled up to dry. In spite of the increasing use of advanced technology for locating schools of fishes, true commercial fishing operations use the same traditional techniques based on three fundamental components—people, boats, and nets.

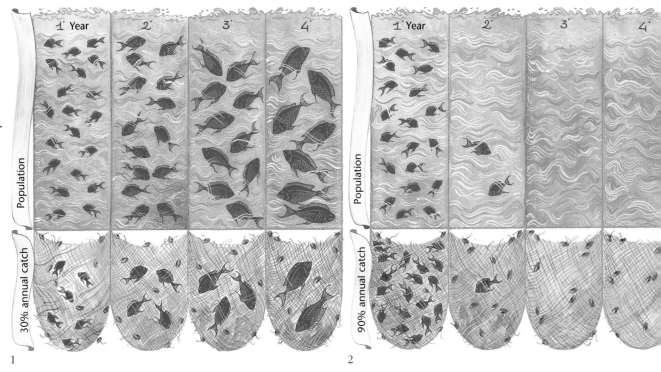

1   2

GLOSSARY

abiotic Term meaning "without life" or nonliving. Abiotic features are all the nonliving components of an organism's *environment*, such as soil, water, and air.

algae Aquatic, plantlike protists capable of *photosynthesis*. Multicellular algae (green, red, and brown) are generally visible to the unaided eye. Unlike plants, algae do not have roots, a stem, or leaves, but instead a single body called a thallus. Microscopic single-celled algae (e.g., diatoms) are an essential part of *phytoplankton*.

arthropods *Phylum* of invertebrates that have a rigid external body case (exoskeleton), a segmented body (*metameria*), and jointed appendages. This group includes the *trilobites*, the merostomates (*Limulus* spp.), the *pycnogonids*, the *crustaceans*, and the insects.

ascidians Primitive chordates (close to vertebrates) that are usually barrel-shaped, gelatinous, and living in coastal waters. Adult ascidians are *sessile;* the *larvae* resemble microscopic tadpoles having tails and a *notochord*.

barnacles Small, colonial crustaceans that have a calcerous shell, which they attach to rocks, the shells of sea turtles, or the fins of whales.

benthos Aquatic organisms that live fixed to the sea floor (e.g., sponges, oysters, and corals) or that move or swim freely near the sea floor (e.g., sea stars, soles, rays).

biodiversity The variety of living things according to the following factors—(a) wealth of species, (b) genetic variability within each species, and (c) the diversity of the *ecosystems* that make up the natural environments of Earth.

biosphere The part of Earth that supports all living things.

biotic community All the living things (organisms) in an *ecosystem*. In the broadest sense, the biotic community is all living things in the *environment*.

bivalves Class of aquatic mollusks with shells having two hinged halves (e.g., mussels, oysters).

brachiopods *Phylum* of *sessile* marine *bivalves*. Brachiopods first appeared in the Cambrian Period and were common in the Palaeozoic and Mesozoic Eras. Around 30,000 fossil species are known; about 250 species exist.

cephalopods Class of tentacled marine *mollusks* adapted to a highly mobile lifestyle. The class includes cuttlefish, squids, octopuses, and the nautiloids (cephalopods with an external shell). In most cephalopods, the shell is absent or reduced to a small internal residue.

chaetognaths *Phylum* of marine invertebrates that are common components of *zooplankton*. They are known as "arrow worms," are predators, are a few centimeters in length, and have transparent bodies and heads with hooked spines.

cnidarians *Phylum* of ancient, essentially marine invertebrates that have mouths that open into a saclike, digestive cavity (the coelenteron). Polyp-cnidarians are sessile and have a trunklike body with a crown of tentacles turned upward. They live fixed to the sea floor, often in colonies (e.g., sea anemones, corals, and madrepores). Medusas (e.g., jellyfishes) are umbrella-shaped, have tentacles facing downward, and swim freely, conducting a solitary lifestyle.

competition Ecological relationship between two species that partly occupy the same *ecological niche* in order to obtain a resource available in limited quantities that is necessary to both.

consumers Organisms that feed on other organisms. In the sea, the primary consumers are those that feed on *phytoplankton* and are generally organisms composing the *zooplankton*. Secondary consumers include the fishes that feed on zooplankton.

copepods Subclass of tiny marine and freshwater crustaceans. Copepods live as

parasites of fishes or as independent organisms. In the latter form, they are perhaps the most important group of *zooplankton* organisms.

crustaceans Class of *arthropods* equipped with antennae, mandibles, maxillae, and compound eyes. The class is composed of many marine and freshwater species, including crabs, prawns, lobsters, and hermit crabs.

ctenophores *Phylum* of carnivorous marine invertebrates closely related to the *cnidarians*. They move with the aid of eight ciliated bands.

division Classification grouping below the kingdom level (equivalent to *phylum*) used for plants and fungi. Those in the same division share certain general anatomical structures. Today scientists tend to define divisions underlining their common ancestral and evolutionary origins.

echinoderms *Phylum* of marine invertebrates that have a calcareous external skeleton covered with skin (often having spines) and tube feet with suckers that can be inflated with water. The five classes of echinoderms include the Echinoidea (sea urchins), Asteroidea (sea stars), Ophiuroidea (brittle-stars), Crinoidea (sea lilies), and Oloturoidea (sea cucumbers).

ecological niche The role of an organism within an *ecosystem*. In practice, it is the "job" performed by that organism within a *biotic community*.

ecosystem The groups of organisms of different species that compose a *biotic community* along with the *abiotic* features of the *environment* with which they interact.

environment An organism's surroundings, and all of the elements, both biotic and abiotic, making up those surroundings.

Euphausiacea An order of *crustaceans* composing the *krill*.

food pyramid Hierarchy of relationships concerning the circulation of matter and the transfer of energy within an *ecosys-*

tem. At the base of the pyramid are the most numerous organisms, the *producers*, then *consumers* (primary consumers, or herbivores), then the consumers of herbivores (secondary consumers, or carnivores), and lastly the consumers of carnivores (tertiary consumers, or super-predators). Organisms become less numerous the higher their position in the pyramid.

gastropods Class of *mollusks* with or without single shells, both terrestrial (snails and slugs) and aquatic (freshwater or marine), such as murices, cowries, and sea-ears. They are characterized by clearly defined heads and a broad, flat foot suited to crawling.

habitat The place in which an organism lives; its "home" within the *environment*.

hermaphroditism The presence of both male and female sexual organs in the same individual.

intertidal zone Part of the marine *ecosystem* between the high-water mark and low-water mark.

krill Small shrimps (*Euphasia superba*) present in the waters of the Antarctic Ocean. They feed on *plankton*, and are an important food resource for whales, seals, penguins, and fishes.

larva (plural is "larvae") Stage in the development of many invertebrates and vertebrates that extends from the hatching of the egg through the completion of the reorganization necessary for transformation into adult form.

metameria Structuring of the body into several successive segments with similar characteristics (e.g., annelids).

mollusks *Phylum* of aquatic and terrestrial invertebrates composed of many species, which are remarkably varied in appearance. All mollusks, however, have a "mantle" of soft tissue that covers the "visceral mass" and a "foot," also composed of soft tissue, used for moving. In many cases the mantle secretes a shell that may be external (e.g., oysters, water snails, nautilus) or internal (cuttlefish). The best-known classes are the *bivalves*, the *cephalopods*, and the *gastropods*.

nekton Aquatic organisms able to oppose the motion of waves, currents, and tides by swimming. They move freely through the water (e.g., fishes, dolphins, whales).

neptunegrass Angiosperm (flowering) plant of the Potamogetonaceae family.

neritic zone The part of the ocean between the low tide mark and a depth of about 200 meters (656 ft).

neuston Aquatic organisms that rest or swim on the surface of the sea (e.g., sea birds, seals, sea turtles).

notochord Semi-rigid supporting structure that forms the backbones of vertebrates.

oceanic zone Part of the marine *ecosystem* composed of the deep ocean (that having a depth greater than 200 meters [656 ft]), or the open ocean.

parasite Organism that lives on a host organism of a different species, using it as shelter, as a source of food, or for other purposes. The damage to the host varies from modest to death.

parasitism Relationship between two organisms in which one (the *parasite*) lives on or in the body tissues or the other (the host).

pelagic Of the open sea (from the Greek *pelagos*).

photic zone Vertical section through the sea within which organisms receive light from the sun (to a depth of 200 meters [656 ft]).

photophore Luminous organ in the skin of many deep sea fishes. It may secrete a chemical that emits flashes of light when activated or may contain colonies of phosphorescent bacteria.

photosynthesis Process of plants, and some chlorophyll-containing bacteria (cyanobacteria) and protists (*algae*), in which inorganic substances supplied by the environment (carbon dioxide and water) are converted into organic substances needed for life (sugars) using sunlight as a source of energy.

phylum (Plural is "phyla") Classification grouping below the kingdom level that is used for large groups of animals, protozoa, bacteria, and sometimes plants and fungi. Organisms in the same phyla are characterized by certain general anatomical structures. Today scientists tend to define phyla underlining their common ancestral and evolutionary origins.

phytoplankton Vegetal *plankton* composed of microscopic, single-celled aquatic organisms capable of *photosynthesis* (the diatoms and dinoflagellates) that live in shallow water where sunlight can penetrate. Organisms of the phytoplankton are *producers*.

plankton Microscopic or small aquatic organisms with limited swimming ability that drift freely without being able to oppose waves, currents, or tides. Plankton is a food source for swimming animals that filter the organism from the water. Divided into *phytoplankton* and *zooplankton*.

Polychaeta Class of marine invertebrates known as annelids that includes the terrestrial earthworms and leeches. They are characterized by *metameria*, numerous tufts of bristles and a worm-like shape.

predation Ecological relationship in which one organism captures, kills, and consumes an organism of a different species.

producers Organisms capable of producing sugars through *photosynthesis*. In the sea these organisms are the *algae* and *phytoplankton*.

pycnogonids Class of arthropods also known as sea spiders.

sessile Organisms that live permanently attached to a solid support.

siphon Tubelike organ of *bivalves* used for taking in and eliminating water and its dissolved substances. Organisms having siphons often live by burrowing into the sea floor with only their siphons extending above the floor's surface.

sponges *Phylum* of simple, *sessile*, marine invertebrates whose cells are not organized into tissues or organs. Their body has many openings—pores (giving the *phylum* the name Porifera), canals, and chambers—through which water flows.

symbiosis Relationship between two organisms of different species that derive advantages from living in close contact with each other.

swim bladder Thin-walled sac filled with air in the abdominal cavity of bony fishes that allows their buoyancy to be maintained and adjusted.

trilobites Extinct class of marine arthropods that lived from the Cambrian Period until the end of the Palaeozoic Era. Their flattened oval body, with two antennae and many pairs of gills and legs, had a robust and compact chitinous back-plate.

zooplankton Animal-like *plankton* composed of a great variety of marine organisms, ranging from microscopic protozoa (foraminifers, radiolarians) and *larvae* of *crustaceans* to small *crustaceans* (jellyfishes). Zooplankton are located on the second level of the marine-food pyramid and are primary consumers that feed on *phytoplankton*.

FURTHER READING

Baines, John D. *Protecting the Oceans*. (Conserving Our World Series). Raintree Steck-Vaughn, 1990

Boyer, Robert E. *Oceanography* (2nd edition). Hubbard Science, 1987

Bramwell, Martyn. *The Oceans* (revised edition). Watts, 1994

Brooks, Felicity. *Seas and Oceans*. (Understanding Geography Series). EDC Publishing, 1987

Conway, Lorraine. *Oceanography*. Good Apple, 1982

Editors, Raintree Steck-Vaughn. *The Raintree Steck-Vaughn Illustrated Science Encyclopedia* (1997 edition). (24 volumes). Raintree Steck-Vaughn, 1997

Fine, John C. *Oceans in Peril*. Simon and Schuster, 1987

Fodor, R. V. *The Strange World of Deep-Sea Vents*. (Earth Processes Series). Enslow Publishers, 1991

Lambert, David. *The Pacific Ocean*. (Seas and Oceans Series). Raintree Steck-Vaughn, 1996

Lambert, David and McConnell, Anita. *Seas and Oceans*. (World of Science Series). Facts on File, 1985

MacRae-Campbell, Linda, et al. *The Ocean Crisis*. (Our Only Earth Series). Zephyr Press, 1990

Markle, Sandra. *Pioneering Ocean Depths*. Simon and Schuster, 1994

Mattson, Robert A. *The Living Ocean*. (Living World Series). Enslow Publishers, 1991

Morgan, Nina. *The Caribbean and the Gulf of Mexico*. (Seas and Oceans Series). Raintree Steck-Vaughn, 1996

———. *The North Sea and the Baltic Sea*. (Seas and Oceans Series). Raintree Steck-Vaughn, 1996

Naden, Corinne J. and Blue, Rose. *The Black Sea*. (Wonders of the World Series). Raintree Steck-Vaughn, 1995

Neal, Philip. *The Oceans*. (Conservation 2000 Series). Trafalgar, 1993

Pifer, Joanne. *EarthWise: Earth's Oceans*. (EarthWise Series). WP Press, 1992

Tesar, Jenny. *Threatened Oceans*. (Our Fragile Planet Series). Facts on File, 1992

Waterlow, Julia. *The Atlantic Ocean*. (Seas and Oceans Series). Raintree Steck-Vaughn, 1996

INDEX